MW01137410

Suffering

....

When Life Falls Apart

Steve Brown

New
Growth
Press

newgrowthpress.com

New Growth Press, Greensboro, NC 27404
www.newgrowthpress.com
Copyright © 2016 by Key Life

Cover Design: Tandem Creative, Tom Temple, tandemcreative.net
Typesetting: Lisa Parnell, lparnell.com

ISBN: 978-1-942572-47-3 (Print)
ISBN: 978-1-942572-48-0 (eBook)

Library of Congress Cataloging-in-Publication Data
    Names: Brown, Stephen W., author.
    Title: Suffering : when life falls apart / Steve Brown.
    Description: Greensboro, NC : New Growth Press, 2016.
    Identifiers: LCCN 2015040564 | ISBN 9781942572473 (print) | ISBN 9781942572480 (ebook)
    Subjects: LCSH: Suffering—Religious aspects—Christianity. | Consolation.
    Classification: LCC BV4909 .B76 2016 | DDC 248.8/6—dc23
    LC record available at http://lccn.loc.gov/2015040564

Printed in India

26 25 24 23 22 21 20 19   3 4 5 6 7

Do you feel like your world is falling apart? Perhaps you are experiencing a family breakdown, a terminal illness, a financial mess, or an emotional problem. Are you going through difficult and devastating circumstances over which you have little control, circumstances that threaten to completely engulf you?

Perhaps you feel like a friend of mine who had just found out that her son had an incurable disease. Her mother-in-law, in an attempt to comfort her, said, "It will all be fine." My friend said that she cried out, "It will never be fine again." If that is the way you feel right now, then this minibook is for you.

Where do you turn when you experience life-altering, it-will-never-be-fine-again circumstances? When life falls apart, I can tell you from experience that the best place to turn is to Jesus, a man of sorrows, who, like you, became well-acquainted with suffering during his time on earth (Isaiah 53:3). As you get to know him, as you sit at his feet, as you walk with him through the storm you are experiencing, life won't ever be the same, but you will find hope, peace, and comfort in the middle of the suffering you are experiencing.

Jesus Understands Suffering Firsthand

The garden of Gethsemane gives us a graphic picture of the suffering that Jesus faced while he was here on earth. What happens in the garden is among the most personal and sensitive portrayals of Jesus Christ in the entire Bible. It is in the garden that Jesus faces his imminent and terrible death on the cross. His community has turned on him. One of his friends has already betrayed him. Even his close friends Peter, James, and John refuse to stand by him. They can't even stay awake as Jesus pleads with his Father to "take this cup away from Me" (Mark 14:36).

Watching how Jesus deals with his painful circumstances gives us a road map for facing our own suffering—a map that includes realism, honesty, and trust in his heavenly Father's goodness in the midst of overwhelming sorrow. So sit with Jesus in the garden for a moment. Things will never be the same, but there is hope for you and yours.

1. Notice the realism of Jesus in dealing with his terribly painful circumstances. Jesus didn't hide what was happening to him. Rather, he was "troubled and deeply distressed," saying to those with him, "My soul is exceedingly sorrowful, even to death" (Mark 14:33–34). We don't know all of what Jesus went through at this time. Part of it was the fear of death and physical suffering. Part of it was that, on the cross, Jesus was soon to be separated from the Father because of our sins. Whatever the full extent of Christ's pain, something went on deep inside that was supernatural and simply horrible . . . something that no man or woman before or since can even begin to comprehend.

There are two great dangers in the Christian life. The first is to build mountains where there are no mountains. The second is to pretend there are no mountains when there are mountains. We are dealing here with the second of those dangers. Christians simply don't call lions *kitties*. Christians simply don't call cancer *indigestion*. Christians simply don't call divorce *trial separation*. The point is this: Jesus refused to look at life and at his situation through rose-colored glasses. In the garden, Jesus faced the reality of his suffering. We should too. Dealing with your suffering starts with acknowledging that it is real, painful, and hard. Pretending everything is okay when your world is falling apart will keep you from going to the Father and crying for help as Jesus did. In his suffering, Jesus goes straight to the one he trusts and loves—his heavenly Father.

2. *Notice the request of Jesus in dealing with his terribly painful circumstances:* "Abba, Father, all things are possible for You. Take this cup

away from Me . . ." (verse 36). A while ago, I talked to a man who said, "When I pray, I don't ask the Father for anything anymore. I simply tell him I want what he wants." That sounds very spiritual, but, the truth is, it's not very realistic. If God is your Father and you're hurting, then you ought to ask. Anything big enough to trouble you is big enough to trouble the Father. Jesus didn't say, "Father, I'm going to leave this whole thing up to you." What did Jesus say? He said, in essence, "Father, I'm scared! Get me out of this mess."

If you have problems, for God's sake, ask him to intervene and to change the circumstances. That is your privilege as a child of the King of the Universe. If you belong to the Father, according to John 1:12, you can go to him. It is the Father's joy to listen to our prayers. Often he says yes.

Years ago I worked for John Holiday at the Holiday Broadcasting Corporation. For weeks I tried to work up my courage to ask him for a raise. Finally, I went into John Holiday's office. There he sat behind his big desk. I said, "Uh . . . I'd like to . . . uh . . . to ask you about something." John Holiday looked up and said, "You've come to ask me for a raise, haven't you?" I said, "Yes, sir." He said, "I was waiting for you. I would have given you a raise weeks ago if you had only asked." We can ask.

3. Notice the reflection of Jesus in dealing with his terribly painful circumstances. "And He said, 'Abba, Father'" (verse 36). Jesus says *Father* twice. It is more significant than it first appears. Jesus says it once in Aramaic and once in Greek. In other words, Jesus repeats himself in two languages, as if to emphasize something very important, the fact that *his Father* is universally in charge of all that happens.

Jesus knew that his loving Father is in control and in charge of all things—including the suffering he was facing. Jesus, the author of the Bible, already knew that Romans 8:28 is true. "And we know that all things work together for good to those who love God, to those who are the called according to His purpose."

Jesus reflected on his position as the Son and on his position under the sovereignty of God. In his double way of calling God the Father, Jesus reflected on a worldview that said the circumstances of life are not just happenstance. God has not gone away on vacation. God is not unaware of our suffering. And if God knows, if he is in control, and if he is our Father, then whatever else happens does not change the truth of God's love, care, and good purposes. Having a loving Father in control of all circumstances means that our suffering is not meaningless or random. God, our Father, is at work in all things.

A while back, I was in the library of a man who wasn't there. A friend of mine stood watching as I looked at the titles of the books and made the observation, "You can always tell a lot about a man by the books that he reads." That's true.

It is also true that you can tell a lot about how a man or woman will handle circumstances by finding out what they believe about the world, God, and themselves. You can tell that Jesus, in the midst of great suffering, believed that his Father in heaven was in control. As he did so, he reflected God. Who do you reflect? If you are a Christian, you reflect your Father, God himself, who is sovereign.

4. *Finally, notice the relinquishment of Jesus in dealing with his terribly painful circumstances.* "Nevertheless, not what I will, but what You will" (verse 36). Jesus faced the most horrible pain and the most horrible death with overtones of supernatural fear than any of us can imagine. He did it for us. The question is, how did he face all of that? Jesus had realistically faced the circumstances. Jesus had made his request to the Father (and the Father said no). From that place Jesus said, "Father, it's okay. I relinquish it to you."

When all has been tried and you can no longer do anything, the principle is simply relinquishment, turning your circumstances over to

God and trusting him to bring you out of the darkness in his way and in his time.

The Tusculani, a people of Italy, once offended the Romans. That was an extremely dangerous thing to do because the Roman power was so great they could easily wipe out any small group. As the Roman armies approached, the Tusculani decided upon a way to deal with them. Rather than fight, they opened the gates of their city. The men of the city unlocked all of their shops and homes. Every man, woman, and child in that city went about their daily business.

When Camillus, the General of the attacking army, reached the city, he was absolutely dumbfounded. The General stood in the town square and said, "You only, of all people, have found out the true method of abating the Roman fury. Your submission has proved your best defense. Upon these terms, we can no more find it in our heart to injure you than upon other terms you could have found power to oppose us."

Circumstances have a way of being like those Romans. Once you decide to no longer fight, but rather, to relinquish those circumstances to your Father God, the ability of circumstances to devastate is devastated. While your circumstances may not change, as you surrender your plans, hopes, and dreams to your Father in heaven, you will see something amazing happen—not overnight of course, but crosses do have a strange way of becoming crowns. How does that happen? It happens as you walk the hard road that Jesus walked, with Jesus alongside you.

The Hard Road

Jesus calls us, as his followers, to walk the same way that he walked. And that's a very hard road. In Mark 8:34–9:1, Jesus realized how little the disciples understood of his ministry. They, like us, figured that following Jesus was a sure way to health, wealth, and happiness. It was within this context of misunderstanding that Jesus gave his hard teaching on discipleship.

Jesus says, "I'm not calling you to a party, but to a purging. I'm not calling you to a comedy, but to a contest. I'm not calling you to a blast, but to a battle in which everything is at stake." The teaching here is actually an expanding sentence. Here is how Jesus explains life with him:

> "Whoever desires to come after Me, let him deny himself, and take up his cross, and follow Me. . . . For whoever is ashamed of Me and My words in this adulterous and sinful generation, of him the Son of Man also will be ashamed when He comes in the glory of His Father with the holy angels." (verses 34, 38)

I don't know about you, but I don't like those words one bit. It would have been easier had Jesus promised Peter a successful fishing business and the disciples self-fulfillment, prestige, and power. But Jesus was not a conman—he was the truth. His business was to tell the truth. That's why he wants his disciples to hear loud and clear, "Deny yourself, take up your cross, and follow me down a way which will be narrow and difficult."

When Garibaldi, the Italian patriot of the nineteenth century who led the fight to unify Italy, told his troops what he expected of them, they replied, "Well, General, what are you going to give us for all this?" Garibaldi answered, "I don't know what you will get except for hunger, cold, wounds, and death." The men stood, quietly considering his words, and then as if one man, they threw up their arms and shouted, "We are the men!" Why did they say such a thing? Because they were inspired both by their leader and by their goal of bringing Italy together. Jesus does inspire us, but even more, he is our only hope. He is the way, the truth, and the life. There is no life without him, and that's news worth sharing—and worth suffering for.

I believe we as Christians have grievously erred in offering to the world an insipid, watered-down, happy-go-lucky, Disney World Christianity. We have taken the challenge, the nails, the blood, the sweat, and the tears out of Christianity. And then we're actually surprised when it wilts before secularism, materialism, and tough circumstances. What did we expect?

Jesus teaches the disciples and us that if we want to go to a tea party, we should go somewhere else. If you want to play games, go somewhere else. Jesus calls us to turn the world upside down. We are called to build a kingdom, and that comes at great cost.

Denying oneself, taking up one's cross, and following Jesus Christ is radical Christianity. And, in the modern world, only radical Christianity can make a difference.

We walk the same road as Jesus, with Jesus

Jesus calls his disciples to walk a very hard road marked earlier by his own footsteps. "And He began to teach them that the Son of Man must suffer many things, and be rejected by the elders and chief priests and scribes, and be killed, and after three days rise again" (verse 31). Jesus is asking us to follow his footsteps. He is not asking us to do something he has not already done.

Sometimes when I'm strongly tempted, I cry out to him. Sometimes when I've done the best I can and everyone has misunderstood, I cry out to him. Sometimes when I'm tired, lonely, and afraid, I cry out to him. And he always responds with "I know." The day will come when I lay my life down and face death head-on, crying out to him. And again he will respond "I know." Jesus identifies. Jesus understands, and because he understands, he sympathizes. "For we do not have a High Priest who cannot sympathize with our weaknesses, but was in all points tempted as we are, yet without sin" (Hebrews 4:15).

Jesus Christ is not the kind of commander who stands on the hillside, pointing us to the battle. He is one who has gone before and who bids us follow. The road would be impossible were it not for the footprints—his footprints.

We walk the same road as Jesus, with Jesus, toward life

Jesus calls us to walk a very hard road marked earlier by his own footprints, which end in eternal life. "For whoever desires to save his life will lose it, but whoever loses his life for My sake and the gospel's will save it. For what will it profit a man if he gains the whole world, and loses his own soul?" (verses 35–36).

If you are looking for self-fulfillment, self-preservation, and self-satisfaction, God will say, "Go ahead. Your reward is in this life." But, if you want to live forever, the call is to deny yourself, to take up a cross, and to follow him. Then, when the time comes, you will find that there is a very high trade-in value on a cross. You trade your cross for glory. You trade your losses for life forever with the Lover of your soul. You trade your tears for joy. You trade your faith for sight.

Life can be more than getting up every morning to check the obituary column and see if you're listed there. God has called you to more and the dividends are something to behold.

Cyrus the conqueror thought that he would live forever. After his conquests, Cyrus offered a great reward for anyone who could give him a new pleasure. Just before he died, Cyrus wrote this epithet for his monument: "I am Cyrus. I occupied the Persian Empire. I was king over Asia . . . Begrudge me not this monument." How sad. That is all he got.

Jesus offers more to those who would walk behind him and with him down the hard road. He says, "Let not your heart be troubled; you believe in God, believe also in Me. In My Father's house are many mansions; if it were not so, I would have told you. I go to prepare a place for you" (John 14:1–2). What are you living for? If you lose your life for Christ's sake, you will save it.

We walk a hard road . . . but we gain, not lose, our souls in the process. Because of that, our suffering has meaning and purpose. We are walking as Jesus walked, with Jesus right beside us, and, just as Jesus's suffering had meaning and purpose, so does ours. Those purposes might not be revealed until we reach heaven, but they are there. The promise and hope of the Bible is that all that happens to us is working toward an ultimate good end (Romans 8:28).

Five Truths that Bring Comfort in Suffering

Sometimes when you are suffering it's helpful to have some concrete things to remember and think about. The familiar story of the disciples in the middle of a storm at sea gives us five important truths about Jesus that will bring his comfort to you in the midst of your suffering (Mark 6:45–52).

1. God is aware of your suffering. Picture the scene. The disciples are dealing with a storm. As far as they know, Jesus is still back with the crowd doing his own thing and totally unaware of what's happening to them. In reality, that's not the case. "Now when evening came, the boat was in the middle of the sea; and He was alone on the land. Then He saw them straining at rowing, for the wind was against them" (verses 47–48).

The fact is, Jesus knew all about how his disciples were struggling and he is aware of every place and everything you go through as a Christian. Don't forget that. Suffering is so much harder to bear if you think God doesn't know and doesn't care. He knows. He cares.

Years ago I received a letter from a girl who had recently had a suicide in her family. Her pain in the letter is just as real today as it was then. In part, she wrote,

> To get to the point (whatever it is) I am so lonely, I'm getting to the point where I'm almost panicky with depression. I feel alone, alone, alone. And grief is about the only emotion I possess apart from an unexplainable anger. I feel hateful and hatred. Last night my mother told me if she had it to do over again, she wouldn't have any kids. She was serious. And I don't blame her. I wish she hadn't too.

Do you know what I told this friend? I told her how the psalmist said that when your parents kick you out, the Lord takes you in. I told her that even if she didn't sense it, and even if she didn't know it, Jesus Christ was aware of everything she was going through.

Once as Augustine and his mother prepared for a long journey home, Augustine expressed the fear that his mother, Monica, would die away from home. She replied, "No one, my son, is ever far from God. I won't die far from home." That is the point. Forget it and it will magnify your problems; remember it and it will keep your problems in perspective.

In Thornton Wilder's *Our Town*, the minister sends a letter to Jane Crofut at her address: "Jane Crofut; The Crofut Farm; Grover's Corners; Sutton County; New Hampshire; United States of America; Continent of North America; Western Hemisphere; The Earth; The Solar System; The Universe; The Mind of God." We are *always* in the mind of God. He knows. He cares.

2. God can change your perspective on your suffering. It was the fourth watch before Jesus went out into the sea to do anything about the storm the disciples were in, sometime between three and six in the morning. In other words, Jesus sat on the mountain, looked at the storm and at the disciples in the storm . . . and he didn't do anything for hours. In fact, he "would have passed them by" (verse 48). Jesus looked at them and knew they were having trouble. He knew they had to row hard, but he also knew they were not going to go down.

Someone tells the story about a man who was walking across a railroad trestle during a very dark night when, horror of horrors, he heard a train coming and had no place to go. The man jumped to the side of the bridge and held on to the edge of the trestle. When the train finally passed by him, the man found he simply didn't have the strength to pull himself up and knew he was just going to hang there. If not, he feared he would fall into the abyss thousands of feet below. The following morning, in the light of day, the man found he was hanging only six inches from the ground!

Sometimes we are like that. We panic, but forget that God has already planned our rescue. The disciples saw it when they saw Jesus. So ask God to show you Jesus in the midst of your suffering. He is your way of escape. He is the ground only six inches under you. He will catch you if you fall.

The message of Scripture to the Christian is this: God is your Father and you can trust him. Jesus is with you, and he is not leaving. The Spirit is present in every moment of your day. Nothing is going to happen to you, period, where you will be left hanging in the night. Ask for faith to see Jesus and the answer will always be yes. The old saying is true, "Fear knocked at the door, faith answered and nobody was there."

3. *God is sovereign and can be trusted in your suffering.* The disciples made their problems worse by confusing the solution with the problem. When they first saw Jesus walking on the

water, the disciples mistook him for a ghost and were terrified. We do that too sometimes. We fail to recognize Jesus when he comes to us in our suffering.

One of the most important principles that any Christian can ever learn is the principle of praise. "In everything give thanks; for this is the will of God in Christ Jesus for you" (1 Thessalonians 5:18). That means that no matter what happens to you, give God the praise. How? You can do it because he is involved in every circumstance of your life.

A little boy went to his grandfather and said, "Granddaddy, do you ever really, I mean *really*, see God?" His grandfather answered, "Son, I sometimes think that's all I see." As Christians, we need, as Brother Lawrence says, to practice the presence of God.

If you want to make your problems worse, see every problem as an accident. If you want to make your problems better, learn to see God's hand in them. Learn to listen carefully and you can hear the words, "Be of good cheer! It is I; do not be afraid" (verse 50).

4. *God has the power and willingness to help you in your suffering.* At first the disciples didn't realize that Jesus was both able and willing to still the storm. Jesus let them experience the power of the storm because he wanted to teach them who

he really is. Only God controls the winds and waves. The disciples needed to know how powerful their friend and teacher is. Knowing that about Jesus changed their perspective on their current situation. The same is true for us today. We all need to know that Jesus Christ controls the winds, whether they are financial, emotional, physical, or spiritual.

Sometimes our problems are made even more difficult because we think we are alone in the wind and the waves, trying our best to figure out how to stay afloat on our own. We think of our own solutions—more money, a different spouse, no spouse . . . our list goes on and on. But the real problem is that we haven't allowed God to be in the boat, and relying on our own solutions keeps him out of the boat. And at that point it is no wonder that as we struggle, our spiritual life struggles too.

Recently my friends gave each kid in their Sunday school class a little plant to take home. Every day the kids were to read their Bibles and pray. Only after reading could they water the plant. Think about it. If the kids didn't read the Bible and didn't pray, the plants weren't watered and eventually died. As they saw what happened to their plants, the kids also saw what happened to their souls and to their lives. Praying and reading the Bible isn't magic and it isn't legalism. It's just the way God has given us to invite him into our lives, into our boats.

As you go to Jesus and talk over everything with him and hear him speak to you in his Word, your heart will be strengthened and helped. The winds won't always cease (and new storms always come), but where Jesus is, his peace rules. And when Jesus is in the boat, the winds cease according to his will and purpose.

5. *God will help you in your present suffering, just as he has helped you in the past.* Take a moment to remember how God has helped, answered, and sustained you through past storms. In their panic, the disciples forgot what they already had seen Jesus do. Look at the end of the story. "And they were greatly amazed in themselves beyond measure, and marveled. For they had not understood about the loaves, because their heart was hardened" (verses 51–52). Our hearts harden too, when we forget about past circumstances and past victories.

The disciples had just seen Jesus feed 5,000 people with five loaves and two fish. Jesus kept breaking the bread and passing it around, and, to top that off, there were twelve full baskets left. Can you believe it? That was the same day the disciples were so frightened about the storm. That is a classic example of a very short memory . . . a problem we often share.

Do you remember the story in Joshua 4? God told the people of Israel to take twelve stones out of the middle of the Jordan River, and to take twelve stones from the side of the bank, and to put them in the middle of the river as an altar. Why was that? When their children would ask, "What do those stones mean?" they could answer, "We are to remember the time when God dried up this riverbed as dry as a bone so that God's people could walk across." We all should be doing that. Keep a journal. Make a list. Tell a friend to remind you. Don't forget how God has helped you in the past as you face your present storm.

The point is this: Life is like an ocean and we're the sailors. Sometimes there are storms; sometimes there are leaky boats; sometimes there seems to be no way out of either. The appropriate prayer for a sailor is: "O God, Thy sea is so great and my boat is so small." Jesus hears your cry for mercy.

Remember my friend who told her mother-in-law "It will never be fine again"? Her son is thirty years old now. As she reflected on the past thirty years she said, "When I thought about the future, I forget to factor in that Jesus would be with us. We went through many hard things

together—chemotherapy, multiple surgeries—
but Jesus was right there with us. He helped. He
sustained. He grew our faith." Her mother-in-
law was right—it was fine. Hard, but fine.

Jesus made all the difference for my friend.
Jesus has made all the difference to me. He will
make all the difference to you too.

Are you tired of
"do more, try harder" religion?

Key Life has only one message, to communicate the radical grace of God to sinners and sufferers. Because of what Jesus has done, God's not mad at you.

On radio, in print, on CDs and online, we're proclaiming the scandalous reality of Jesus' good news of radical grace…leading to radical freedom, infectious joy and surprising faithfulness to Christ.

For all things grace, visit us at **KeyLife.org**